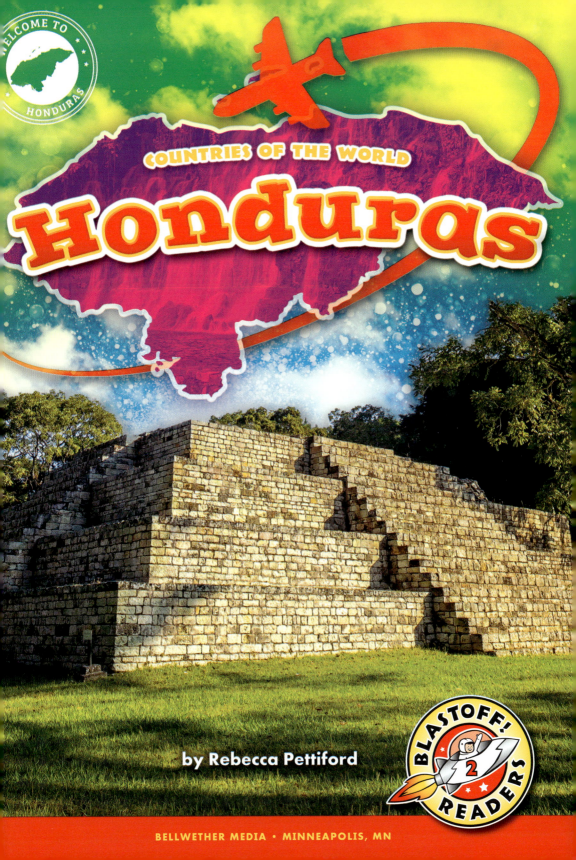

Blastoff! Readers are carefully developed by literacy experts to build reading stamina and move students toward fluency by combining standards-based content with developmentally appropriate text.

Level 1 provides the most support through repetition of high-frequency words, light text, predictable sentence patterns, and strong visual support.

Level 2 offers early readers a bit more challenge through varied sentences, increased text load, and text-supportive special features.

Level 3 advances early-fluent readers toward fluency through increased text load, less reliance on photos, advancing concepts, longer sentences, and more complex special features.

★ **Blastoff! Universe**

Reading Level

Grade K — Grades 1–3 — Grade 4

This edition first published in 2026 by Bellwether Media, Inc.

No part of this publication may be reproduced in whole or in part without written permission of the publisher. For information regarding permission, write to Bellwether Media, Inc., Attention: Permissions Department, 3500 American Blvd W, Suite 150, Bloomington, MN 55431.

Library of Congress Cataloging-in-Publication Data

LC record for Honduras available at: https://lccn.loc.gov/2025014960

Text copyright © 2026 by Bellwether Media, Inc. BLASTOFF! READERS and associated logos are trademarks and/or registered trademarks of Bellwether Media, Inc. Bellwether Media is a division of FlutterBee Education Group.

Editor: Betsy Rathburn   Designer: Laura Sowers

Printed in the United States of America, North Mankato, MN.

Table of Contents

All About Honduras	4
Land and Animals	6
Life in Honduras	12
Honduras Facts	20
Glossary	22
To Learn More	23
Index	24

All About Honduras

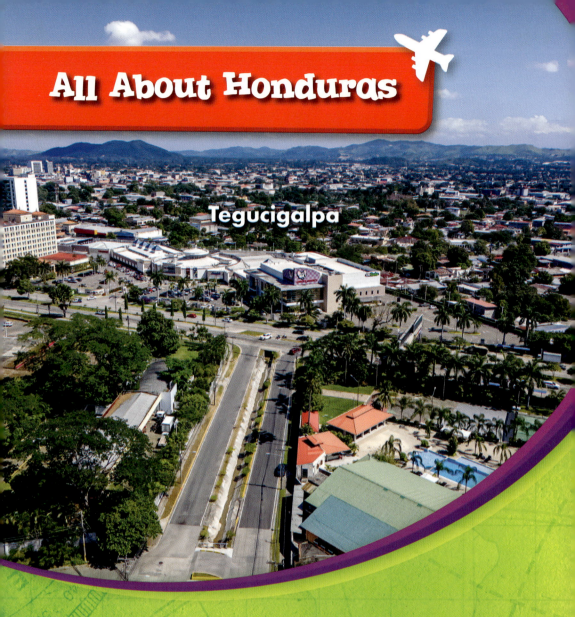

Tegucigalpa

Honduras is the second-largest country in **Central America**.

It is known for its white beaches and **Maya ruins**. Its capital is Tegucigalpa.

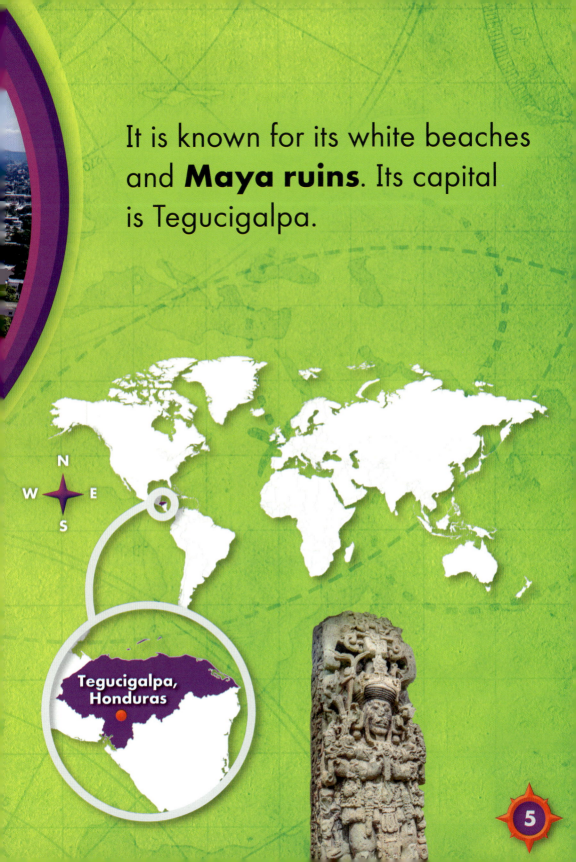

Land and Animals

Mountains cover most of Honduras. **Cloud forests** dot the mountains.

Plains line the coast. **Rain forests** and river valleys are found throughout Honduras.

cloud forest

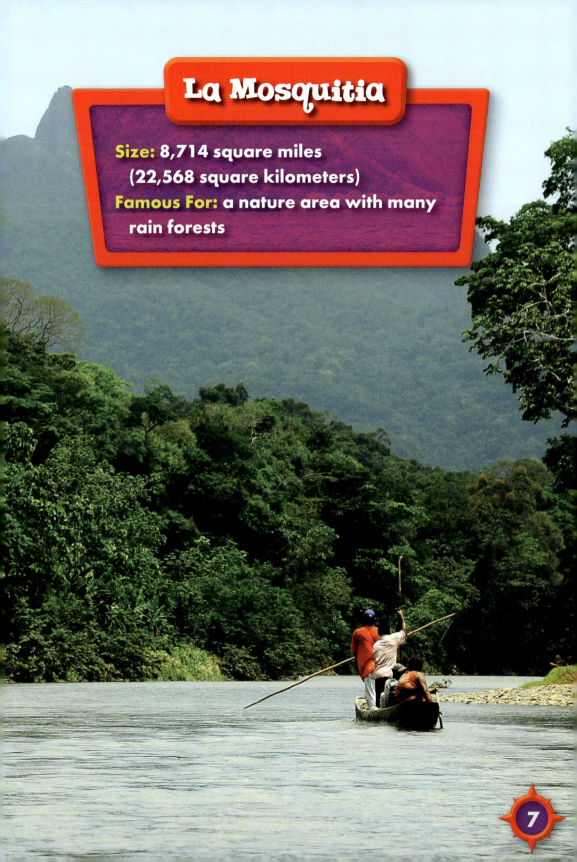

La Mosquitia

Size: 8,714 square miles (22,568 square kilometers)

Famous For: a nature area with many rain forests

Honduras is mostly **tropical**. May to November is the **wet season**.

The rest of the year is dry. The days are warm. It is cooler in the mountains.

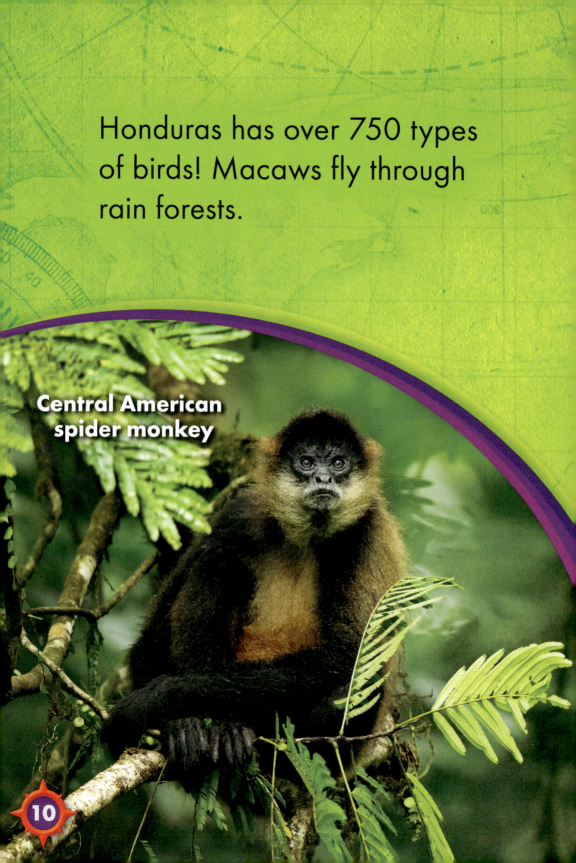

Honduras has over 750 types of birds! Macaws fly through rain forests.

Central American spider monkey

Animals of Honduras

scarlet macaw

jaguarundi

Central American spider monkey

Yucatan white-tailed deer

Jaguarundi climb trees. Monkeys swing from branches. Deer find plants to eat.

Life in Honduras

Most Hondurans have an **Indigenous** and European **background**. They speak Spanish.

Many people live in cities. Most people are **Christians**.

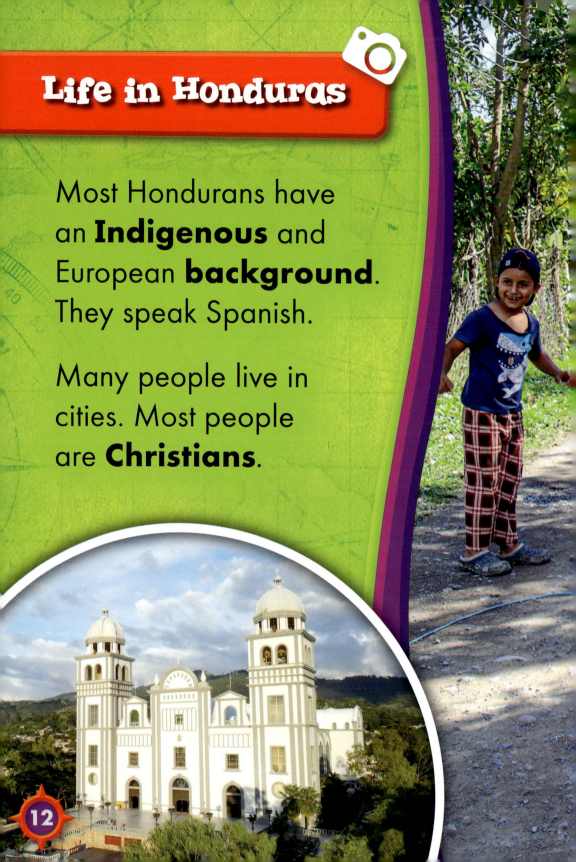

soccer

bird-watching

Hondurans love soccer. Basketball is also popular. Some people like bird-watching and fishing.

People play **traditional** music. They sing and dance.

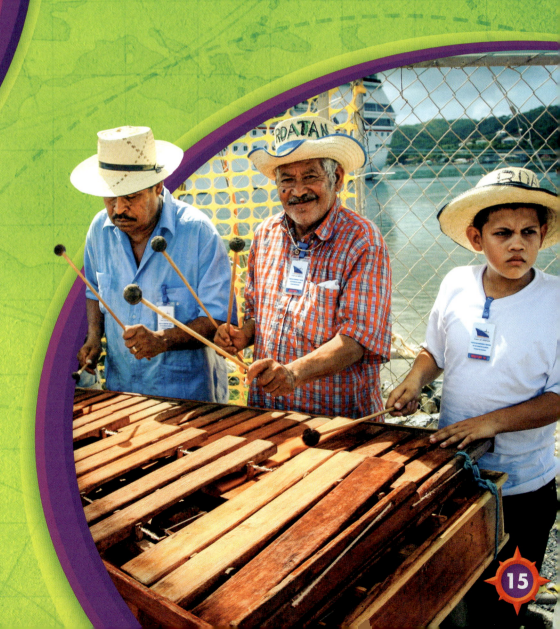

Many meals include tortillas. *Baleadas* are tortillas filled with beans and cheese.

Honduran Foods

tortillas

baleadas

plantain chips

torrejas

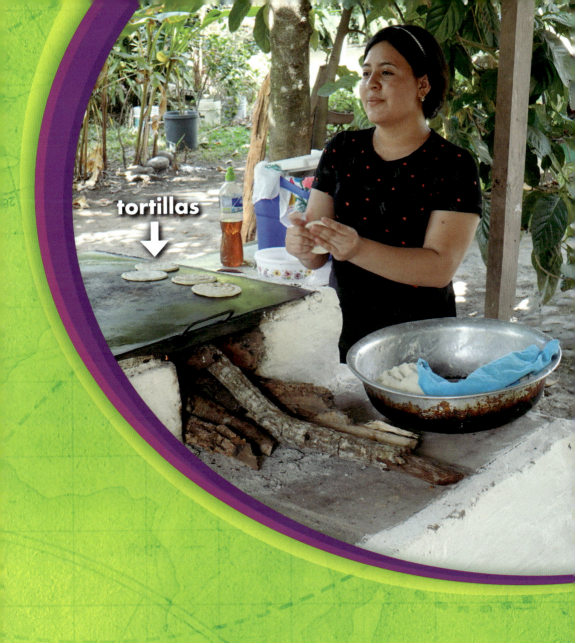

Plantain chips come with many meals. *Torrejas* are a treat!

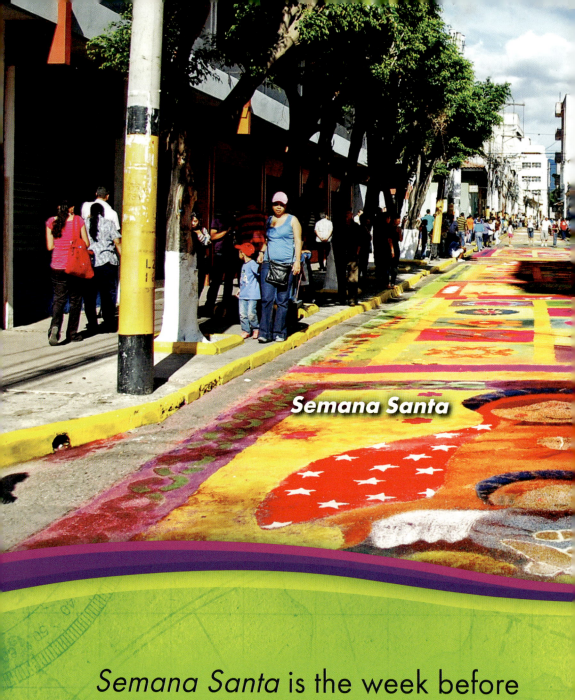

Semana Santa

Semana Santa is the week before Easter. Christians make colorful art on some city streets.

In summer, people **celebrate** Feria Juniana. This big **festival** has parades and fireworks.

Honduras Facts

Size:
43,278 square miles
(112,090 square kilometers)

Population:
9,529,188 (2024)

National Holiday:
Independence Day (September 15)

Main Language:
Spanish

Capital City:
Tegucigalpa

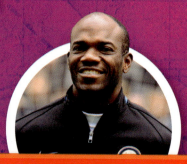

Famous Face

Name: David Suazo

Famous For: former professional soccer player

Religions

- other: 12%
- Evangelical Christian: 55%
- Roman Catholic: 33%

Top Landmarks

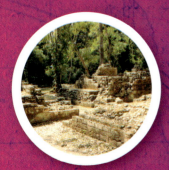
Copán Ruins

Lake Yojoa

Santa Bárbara Fortress

Glossary

background—people's experiences, knowledge, and family history

celebrate—to do something special or fun for an event, occasion, or holiday

Central America—the countries between Mexico and South America

Christians—people who believe in the words of Jesus Christ

cloud forests—mountain forests that are wet and cloudy

festival—a time or event of celebration

Indigenous—related to people originally from an area

Maya ruins—old buildings and other structures left behind by the Maya people

plains—areas of flat land with few trees

rain forests—thick, green forests that receive a lot of rain

traditional—related to customs, ideas, or beliefs handed down from one generation to the next

tropical—having to do with a place that is hot and wet

wet season—a time of year when it rains a lot

To Learn More

AT THE LIBRARY

Barnes, Rachael. *Guatemala*. Minneapolis, Minn.: Bellwether Media, 2023.

Kenney, Karen Latchana. *Rain Forests*. Minneapolis, Minn.: Bellwether Media, 2022.

Peterson, Megan Cooley. *Super Surprising Trivia About Rain Forest Animals*. North Mankato, Minn.: Capstone Press, 2024.

ON THE WEB

FACTSURFER

Factsurfer.com gives you a safe, fun way to find more information.

1. Go to www.factsurfer.com.

2. Enter "Honduras" into the search box and click 🔍.

3. Select your book cover to see a list of related content.

Index

animals, 10, 11
basketball, 14
beaches, 5
bird-watching, 14
capital (see Tegucigalpa)
Central America, 4
Christians, 12, 18
cities, 12, 18
cloud forests, 6
coast, 6
Feria Juniana, 19
fishing, 14
food, 16, 17
Honduras facts, 20–21
La Mosquitia, 7
map, 5
Maya ruins, 5
mountains, 6, 9
music, 15
people, 12, 14, 15, 18, 19

plains, 6
rain forests, 6, 7, 10
river valleys, 6
say hello, 13
Semana Santa, 18
soccer, 14
Spanish, 12, 13
Tegucigalpa, 4, 5
tropical, 8
wet season, 8

The images in this book are reproduced through the courtesy of: Unai Huizi Photography, front cover; erenalkis, p. 3; Gianfranco Vivi, pp. 4-5; Diego Grandi, p. 5; Manuel Chinchilla, p. 6; Nature Picture Library/ Alamy Stock Photo, pp. 6-7; Unai, pp. 8-9; travelphotos, p. 9; Milan, pp. 10-11; Milan Zygmunt, p. 11 (scarlet macaw); Janusz Pienkowski, p. 11 (jaguarundi); ChameleonsEye, p. 11 (Central American spider monkey); Nature's Charm, p. 11 (Yucatan white-tailed deer); marco, p. 12; Omri Eliyahu, pp. 12-13, 21 (Lake Yojoa); ZUMA Press, Inc./ Alamy Stock Photo, p. 14 (bird-watching); Igor Kiporuk, pp. 14-15; pablopicasso, p. 15; hansgeel, p. 16 (tortillas); Elder Diaz, p. 16 (*baleadas*); Sylphien, p. 16 (plantain chips); 3waycolor, p. 16 (*torrejas*); Clive Marshall/ Alamy Stock Photo, p. 17; Lmarc1, pp. 18-19; Rafayel Melik-Israyelyan, p. 20 (flag); Anton_Ivanov, p. 20 (David Suazo); De Kam, p. 21 (Copán Ruins); Renan Greinert, p. 21 (Santa Bárbara Fortress); Passakorn Umpornmaha, p. 23.